The Self, The Other, & God

POEMS

Tricia Barker

First Edition, 2019

Published by Tricia Teaches, LLC

USA

Copyright @ 2019 by Tricia Barker

All rights reserved. No part of this book may be used or reproduced in any manner whatsoever, including Internet usage, without written permission from Tricia Teaches, LLC, expect in the case of brief quotations embodied in critical articles and reviews.

Cover art by Hilary Leehane

Library of Congress Cataloging-in-Publication Data

Names: Barker, Tricia, author.

Title: The Self, The Other, & God: Poems by Tricia Barker

Description: First Edition | Fort Worth: Tricia Teaches, LLC, 2020|

Identifiers ISBN (print): 978-1-7343792-0-4

ISBN (e-book): 978-1-7343792-2-8

Subjects: Poetry, Spirituality

Tricia Teaches, LLC

www.triciabarkernde.com

triciateachesllc@gmail.com

Printed in the United States of America

Advance Praise for The Self, The Other, & God

Each step we take along our path is a step that helps lead us back to the sacred recognition of our eternal essence and nature. What Tricia Barker has done for each of us, in her book *The Self, The Other & God* is to provide a way home to love and gratitude for all that surrounds us each day. Remembering that we are here to create just as the Divine created through love and light is at the heart of Tricia's gift to us in this inspiring and amazing devotional to love and life.

Tricia lays out, in striking detail, the thoughts, emotions and universal fears that inhabit our daily lives, and I guarantee you- you will find yourself shouting, "Yes! She gets me! She knows."

As you embark on this journey into the Spirit of this woman with each page you turn you can feel Tricia's heartbeat. You can peek into the Soul of this being of light. And you can become part and parcel of her experiential knowledge of the Divine.

I have read many books of poetry and prose. "The Self, The Other & God" is destined to become your companion on your journey of discovery to your Divine self.

Dr. Sharon Prentice is a psychologist and the author of *Becoming Starlight: Surviving Grief and Mending the Wounds of Loss*

Dedication

To my students who didn't raise their hands when asked if they liked reading poetry but later picked out poems they enjoyed by Sylvia Plath, Anne Sexton, Langston Hughes, Edgar Allen Poe, Robert Frost, Maya Angelou, or Billy Collins.

To my students who write poems and spent hours in writing workshops talking about life and poetry.

To my students who introduced me to the Instapoets and encouraged me create a collection of work that is straightforward and easily consumable.

To all the people who have an interest in near-death experiences and read my memoir *Angels in the OR: What Dying Taught Me About Healing, Survival, and Transformation* published by Post Hill Press in April 2019.

May you all be blessed!

Table of Contents

~*The Self*~ 1

My radiant body imagines itself 2

My redemption 3

Once, the sounds I made 4

The only thing I have done wrong.............................5

Perhaps the howling 6

One night I stopped time 7

No one is on the road today, ...8

Each catastrophe disappears.....................................9

I'm more joyful than you imagine. 10

Four aces in my hand. 11

I got older and my balance improved. 12

~*The Other*~ 13

I hope he doesn't bellyache 14

A woman wearing a silver shift 15

We might tell a few stories 16

I wanted my man 17

You grew out of red clay hills 18

I have seen you in bars...19

Your journey has brought you 20

When Narcissus left for work 21

Watch their flights and returns 22

You can't call a relationship love 23

I never imagined that 24

Our lives are unnatural 25

Miraculously 26

~*God*~ 27

Occasionally 28

The only true freedom 29

Tell your heart to calm itself 30

Oh Lord, I have slammed 31

We all shuffle off this mortal coil 32

We are all in this together 33

Prepare for what is destined 34

How could I know that the angels 35

If you have memories before birth 36

We are part flight of dove 37

The choice to experience 38

How many galaxies will we locate 39

We came into this world 40

With faith 41

ABOUT THE AUTHOR 42

~The Self~

-1-

My radiant body imagines itself
composed of wild flowers and sinewy grasses
stretching upwards toward the sun,
never imagining anything so strong could die.

-2-

My redemption

did not resemble their kind

never based on the bible belt kind

only on amazing grace

sparrows landing near my table

soft arms of a lover

deep sleep and forgiveness

from the other side

no explanations

and no particular country

for my soul

-3-

Once, the sounds I made

were discordant, rebellious,

roaring down time

with a broken taillight

and squeaky brakes.

Now, I am a vessel of that past

and this present life.

All the elements:

everything light and dark,

miss and hit the mark.

-4-

The only thing I have done wrong

is choosing to be born

with a bright, independent spirit,

and no matter how badly they

wanted to beat it out of me

and call God the devil,

I continued to enjoy my life,

extravagantly, all the more,

despite what they thought

and said about me.

-5-

Perhaps the howling

in my veins is audible,

at times.

-6-

One night I stopped time,

and surveyed my life from a gold-speckled booth

at a 24-hour diner.

The lives around me simmered in smoke.

So much had happened that appeared

unlucky and random.

I realized that I was reaching the point

of more than I could handle

and wondered what might happen next.

-7-

No one is on the road today,

and I know that I am more than this moment.

I am the child who was a sage,

who controlled the wind,

read the stars,

and rode the morning light past the moon.

I am more.

More than the images

people construct of me in their minds.

-8-

Each catastrophe disappears
into the smoke of my mind,
and I remember to forgive,
getting lighter with every death,
wounding, or suppressed memory.
Every nightmare brings me
closer to letting go of suffering,
closer to tranquil dreams of flying
and seeing the world turn golden.

-9-

I'm more joyful than you imagine.
Think sunlight, green pastures, hawks, and eagles.
Think evergreen trees, waterfalls, steep cliffs,
and hidden trails through a forest.
Think hiking by a stream and floating
timeless in a lake.
Think laughter and esoteric study.
Think love, sweet lasting love.
Think better, not bitter, thoughts for me,
for you, and for all of us.

-10-

Four aces in my hand.
Only a couple of lucky days
in my entire chaotic life,
and now everything is moving
like an arrow set aflame.
Instant vibrational love match,
success at work, meaningful hobbies,
supportive friends, good health,
recognition, and wonderful dinners
that I don't have to cook.
Miraculously, my life is almost
as fantastic as my social media profile
makes it appear.

-11-

I got older and my balance improved.

I can stand in tree pose for hours.

I recovered some childhood joy,

retrograded all the way back

to the spark of God

and held on to that spark

like a winning

90-million-dollar lottery ticket.

~The Other~

-12-

I hope he doesn't bellyache

between sips of southern comfort

about some girl who broke his heart

and ruin my fine summer night.

The beautiful ones can't believe

that anyone they want

would ever

leave them.

-13-

A woman, wearing a silver shift,

sat meditating on a small cliff above us.

When she opened her eyes, she saw my boyfriend

bend and spring across a ledge, agile as a deer.

Her smile widened with appreciation

and she winked at me as she shook out

her long, Venusian curls.

-14-

We might tell a few stories,

and our kisses might lead somewhere

later than night, or not,

but our ties to earth

and heaven will be loosened,

long enough to breathe

out molecules of our past and create

an enviable, simple, present tense life.

-15-

I wanted my man to drive the long stretches

of highway and navigate the wide, winding lanes

leading into the future, propelling me, and my dreams

of going somewhere, through the cold nights

and bewildering directions. I wanted to be

two drifters off to see the world...

-16-

You grew out of red clay hills, black tar roads,

bay windows, and loneliness.

You emerged out of the dust on a bookshelf,

a passage from the Psalms,

a beard smelling of smoke, shepherd's clothing,

and verdant meadows.

You sprung from the ground, from cow dung–

your life a hallucination.

You became a plum blossom

falling from a purple tree,

a broken baby bird, thin and gray feathered,

ants marching through its eye sockets.

You learned that to love is to weep.

-17-

I have seen you in bars, mellowed,

left elbow propping your head up,

gloomy, then suddenly glowing and manic,

commanding the world around you,

a general of movement and destinations.

You fought, made love,

and ran stumbling down alleys

all in one night.

-18-

Your journey has brought you

to a blue shag rug,

orange beaded lamp,

beetles on the ceiling, flowers in the tub,

ruffled black bird perched on a streetlight

squawking at the evening star,

white weeds shaken by the wind...

-19-

When Narcissus left for work,

I would put on the sandals he wore

to feel closer to him.

My feet would soak up the remnants of the love

he had for his feet, his body,

and after a while, I realized

that in his mind

I was less important

than the ground he walked upon.

-20-

Watch their flights and returns,
like birds going away to gather twigs.
Pity her as she falls to the floor,
and his red car speeds away
like a huge arrow shot through her.
Wounded. Betrayal. Threats.
She said the wrong thing.
He became too angry.
Fill in whatever you want to fill in.
Returned train tickets.
Even a trip to jail.
Premonitions. Angel's voices.

-21-

You can't call a relationship love

when it ends gruesomely

with police sirens,

fear, or learning to live with it:

daily threats, lack of sleep,

denying love has turned out badly.

-22-

I never imagined that tying my life to another's

would be the equivalent

of following an anchor to the bottom of the sea.

No treasure.

No light.

Just a suffocating ocean.

-23-

Our lives are unnatural transmigrations

from this uncertain world to the next,

and our souls are conglomerates

of slaughtered, wild beauty.

I keep reaching out for the other,

but the other is wounded and blind.

-24-

Miraculously, we found each other

and journeyed across a rocky landscape

to a place of peaceful acceptance.

We found understanding

instead of projection,

companionship alongside passion,

heaven in late-night embraces,

and sweet entanglement

frequently.

~God~

-25-

Occasionally, I allow myself to feel safe

as an ordinary woman, in plain clothes,

all the pain all nicely shored-up,

until the right words penetrate me

and tears jump out of my eyes,

against my will.

There is no one I miss

more than God.

-26-

The only true freedom I have known
is leaving my body in the place it fell,
like a discarded garment.

-27-

Tell your heart to calm itself.
Remember a tall, protective pine tree
you knew and loved as a child.
Remember the silence you walked in
before entering this loud,
incessant den of fear.
Though you are hungry,
and your hands shake,
know that God will guide you home,
even though the darkness.

-28-

Oh Lord, I have slammed doors shut

with superhuman strength,

with centuries of hate and vengeance,

but you keep whispering of a way out

and through these words

I find it.

-29-

We all shuffle off this mortal coil,

and it is a relief,

not a punishment, nothing to fear.

You leave your story on the ground.

You see (finally) how pride

and victimization are the same roles

you fall for every time.

-30-

We are all in this together, not separately,

not in contradiction, not in competition.

You either elevate or deflate,

You either gravitate to the lighter side,

or stagnate in darkness, in the absence of love.

-31-

Prepare for what is destined to be.

The notes of a symphony

will crescendo and fall in a universe

made up of the love inside of you.

There is freedom in truth

and truth in a love that is free and vibrating

across the earth, free as the spirit you will become

and fly into a space I have opened for you now.

-32-

How could I know that the angels

I recalled from paintings

would become bright, intelligent companions

at the end of my bed

and that the torrential light from their eyes

would answer my questions instantly?

-33-

If you have memories before birth

they are of flight,

of colors, of people

who you know now

and laughter.

-34-

We are part flight of dove, part sunset, part rocky cliff

and streams. Don't forget the part of you

that dreams. It will matter more than you think.

I will see you there after this life,

and all will be healed.

-35-

The choice to experience

the eternal

in temporary

fleeting moments

is why we call love

falling.

-36-

How many galaxies will we locate,

and will this help us know God,

or will we, somewhere between

the enormity and the miniscule,

simply close our eyes,

smile, and ride.

-37-

We came into this world

with the Milky Way in the light contained in our eyes

and magic in our tiny fingertips.

All of time was no time.

Beauty multiplied wherever

our gaze landed, and if I had one wish tonight

it would be that everyone could feel harmony–

no empty spaces, no ragged edges,

no knife wounds cutting

through the soul.

Whole.

-38-

With faith, some people have

dared to grab on to the tail of a shooting star

and flown away from their misfortune,

loud as airplanes and quick as startled birds.

They have whipped through the night sky,

their problems and everyone else's

turned to ancient history.

ABOUT THE AUTHOR

Tricia Barker experienced a profound near-death experience during her senior year of college, and this experience guided her to teach overseas, in public schools, and at the college level. Her near-death experience story has been featured on *I Survived: Beyond and Back*, *National Geographic Magazine*, *Simple Grace Magazine*, *Women's World Magazine*, and *The Doctor Oz Show*.

Tricia's memoir, *Angels in the OR: What Dying Taught Me About Healing, Survival, and Transformation* is also available through Audible. This book tells a story of her near-death experience, teaching mission, and eventual triumph over trauma in her past. The book also focuses on the importance being of service to the world and the healing power of giving unconditional love to others. Tricia Barker and a screenwriter have recently completed a screenplay based on her memoir *Angels in the OR*.

Tricia is a graduate of The University of Texas. She also received her MFA in Creative Writing from Goddard College. Currently, she teaches English and Creative Writing at a beautiful community college in Fort Worth, Texas. She interviews other near-death experiencers, researchers, healers, spiritual teachers, and authors on her YouTube Channel. Tricia's poetry and essays have been published in several publications including *The Binnacle*, *The Paterson Literary Review*, and *The Midwest Quarterly*.

Website www.triciabarkernde.com

www.ingramcontent.com/pod-product-compliance
Lightning Source LLC
Chambersburg PA
CBHW032104040426
42449CB00007B/1177